The Crusades
Cumulative Index

The Crusades Cumulative Index

Cumulates Indexes For:
The Crusades: Almanac
The Crusades: Biographies
The Crusades: Primary Sources

Ralph Zerbonia, Index Coordinator

U•X•L
An imprint of Thomson Gale, a part of The Thomson Corporation

THOMSON
GALE

Detroit • New York • San Francisco • San Diego • New Haven, Conn. • Waterville, Maine • London • Munich

THOMSON
GALE

The Crusades Reference Library: Cumulative Index

Project Editor
Ralph Zerbonia

Permissions
Lori Hines, Susan J. Rudolph, William A. Sampson

Imaging and Multimedia
Lezlie Light, Mike Logusz, Kelly A. Quinn

Product Design
Pamela Galbreath, Jennifer Wahi

Composition
Evi Seoud

Manufacturing
Rita Wimberley

For more information, contact:
Thomson Gale
27500 Drake Rd.
Farmington Hills, MI 48331-3535
Or you can visit our Internet site at
http://www.gale.com

Cover photographs reproduced by permission: Saint Louis Leading Army, photograph. © Bettman/Corbis; Richard I, photograph. Courtesy of the Library of Congress; Anna Comnena, illustration. Courtesy of the Library of Congress.

LIBRARY OF CONGRESS CATALOGING-IN-PUBLICATION DATA

The Crusades Reference Library: Cumulative Index / Ralph Zerbonia, index coordinator.
p. cm. — (The Crusades reference library)
ISBN 0-7876-9217-4 (alk. paper)
1. Jones, J. Sydney. Crusades. Biographies—Indexes. 2. O'Neal, Michael J., 1949- Crusades. Almanac—Indexes 3. Crusades. Primary sources—Indexes. 4. Crusades—Juvenile literature—Indexes. 5. Crusades—Biography—Dictionaries, Juvenile—Indexes. 6. Crusades—Sources—Juvenile literature—Indexes. I. Zerbonia, Ralph. II. Series.

Z6207.C97C78 2004
[D157]
016.90907—dc22 2004018002

Printed in the United States of America
10 9 8 7 6 5 4 3 2

ISBN 0-7876-9178-X

Crusades Reference Library Cumulative Index

A = The Crusades: Almanac
B = The Crusades: Biographies
PS = The Crusades: Primary Sources

Bold italic type indicates set titles or literary works. **Bold** entries and page numbers indicate specific biographies in *The Crusades: Biographies,* or a primary source title or author in *The Crusades: Primary Sources.* Illustrations are marked by (ill.).

A

Abbasids
A: 74, 116, 119
Abbot Daniel
PS: 148, **151–54**, 155 (ill.)
Abbot of Cîteaux
A: 64
Abdurrahman
A: 75
Abelard, Peter
B: 60–61
Abu Bakur
A: 71–72
Abu Muhammad
B: 206
Abu Ya'qub Yusuf
B: 31
Acre, fall of
A: 189–91
B: 40, 190
See also **"The Fall of Acre, 1291"**
Adhemar
B: 105, 106
"Ahi! Amours! Com dure departie/Alas, Love, What Hard Leave"
PS: **91–92**
Akhlaq-I-Nasri ("Nairean Ethics")
B: 144
Al-Abiwardi, Abu I-Musaffar
PS: 98, **100–01**
Al-Adil, Malik al-
A: 99–100
B: 130
Al-Aqsa Mosque
A: 14, 22, 88
Al-Din, Nur
A: 93–94, 122–24
See also Nur Al-Din
Al-Harawi
A: 118
Al-Kamil, al-Malik
A: 112
See also Malik al-Kamil; Kamil, al-Malik al-
Al-Khashshab, Abu al-Fadl ibn
A: 79
Al-Mansur
B: 32, 35

Al-Mu'azzam Shams-al-Din Turan-Shah
A: 112
Al-Mustansir
B: 43
Al-Mustazhir Billah
A: 118
Al-Zij-Ilkhani ("The Ilkhanic Tables")
B: 144
Albigensian Crusade
B: 51
Alexiad, The
B: 69–73
***PS:* 15–17**
Alexius I Comnenus
A: 51 (ill.), 52, 56, 84
B: **1–8**, 1 (ill.), 105–108, 168–69, 214
PS: 2, 10
Alexius III
A: 103–05
B: 13, 15
PS: 25–28
Alexius IV (Angelus)
A: 103–05
B: **11–18**, 14 (ill.), 67
PS: 29
Alexius V
A: 105
B: 16
PS: 29
Alfred the Great
A: 9
Ali ibn Abi Talib, Hazrar
A: 72
Alp Arslan
B: 3, **21–28**, 215
Amalric
B: 208
PS: 73
Anacletus II, Pope
B: 59
Angelus, Isaac
A: 103, 105
Anna Comnena
PS: 11 (ill.), **15–17**
See also **Comnena, Anna**
Annales Herbipolenses
***PS:* 108–09**
Antioch
fall of
B: 108
siege of
A: 85–86
PS: 13–18
"Apologia for the Second Crusade"
B: 63
Arab-Syrian Gentleman and Warrior in the Period of the Crusades, An (*Kitab al-I'tibar*)
B: 219, 224–25
Ark of the Covenant
A: 4
Arslan, Kilij
A: 84
Assassins
A: 77–79, 122, 182–83
B: 23, 44, 52, 158, 203–10
Atsiz ibn Abaq
B: 26
Averroës
B: **29–36**, 29 (ill.), 48
Aybek
B: 198–99
Aymeric
***PS:* 72–75**

B

Bagi Seian
PS: 13
Balak
A: 122
Baldwin I
A: 61–62, 84, 89, 90 (ill.) 122
B: 17, 104, 105, 109–10, 115
Baldwin II
A: 122
B: 157
Baldwin III
A: 92 (ill.), 93 (ill.)
B: 155, 159–61
Baldwin of Flanders
A: 105
Barkiyaruq
A: 119
Bartholomew, Peter
A: 85
Battle of Arsuf
A: 99
B: 178, 190
Battle of Ayn Jalut
PS: 139
Battle of Damagan
B: 24
Battle of Harbiya
A: 181
Battle of Hattin
A: 28, 95
Battle of Karbala
A: 73
Battle of las Navas de Tolosa
A: 18
Battle of Mansurah
B: 39, 133
Battle of Manzikert
A: 49
B: 3, 4, 26
PS: 2
Battle of Ponte San Giovanni
B: 85
Battle of Tours
A: 73
Baybars, Ali-Zahir
A: 188–89
B: **37–45**, 143, 197–98
PS: 48–49, 134–140
Benjamin of Tudela
B: **47–56**
PS: 116, **124–30**, 131
Beowulf
A: 170
Bernard of Clairvaux
A: 91, 131–32, 152
B: **57–64**, 57 (ill.), 60 (ill.), 77, 115, 118
PS: 108, 130, 167–68
Blanche of Castile
B: 139–41, 142, 194
Bohemond
A: 84–86
B: 3, 4, 71, 105, 107–08, 110
PS: 14, 15–17, 73, 74
Boniface of Montferrat
B: 14
PS: 25
Book of a Thousand Nights and a Night (Arabian Nights)
PS: 148 (ill.), 162
"Book of Historical Records"
B: 62

Book of the Maghrib
***PS:* 101–03**
Bryennius, Nicephorus
B: 68, 69
Burton, Richard
PS: 158 (ill.), 162
Bush, George W.
A: 201

C

Caliphs, first four
A: 16 (ill.)
"The Capture of Jerusalem"
***PS:* 51–54**
Cathars
A: 63–64
Cathedral of Santa Sophia (Hagia Sophia)
A: 105, 106 (ill.)
Chanson d'Antioch
A: 174
Chanson de geste
A: 171
PS: 79, 82, 94
Chanson de Roland
A: 173–74, 172 (ill.)
See also ***Song of Roland***
Chapel of the Innocents
A: 45
Charlemagne
A: 8–10, 59, 172–73
PS: 80
Charles Martel
A: 8, 17, 59, 73
Chems Eddaulb
PS: 13
Children's Crusade
A: 56–59, 57 (ill.)
PS: 23, 28–31, 30 (ill.), 110
Chivalry
A: 135–38, 143–44
Chrétien de Troyes
A: 178
Christianity
A: 6
PS: 144–45
Chronica Regiae Coloniensis
***PS:* 28–29**
Chronicle of the Fourth Crusade and the Conquest of Constantinople
***PS:* 24–28**
Church of the Ascension
A: 45
Church of the Holy Sepulchre
A: 22, 24–26, 28, 30, 35, 42–45, 89, 112–113
Church of the Nativity
A: 46
Clement III, antipope
B: 213–14
Clement V, Pope
A: 154
Cligès
A: 178
Columbus, Christopher
A: 195–97
Commentary on the Mishnah
B: 148
Comnena, Anna
B: 4, **67–74,** 67 (ill.)
See also Anna Comnena
Conon de Béthune
PS: 81, **91–92**
Conrad, King of Jerusalem
A: 111
Conrad III
A: 66, 91, 92 (ill.), 93 (ill.)
B: 63, 77
Conrad of Montferrat
B: 209
Constantine I
A: 6, 21, 26, 33, 35, 42, 48
B: 12
Constantinople
A: 2, 7, 11–12, 49–52, 67
fall of
A: 103–05, 104 (ill.)
B: 17–18, 18 (ill.)
PS: 24–29
Constitutions of Melfi
B: 99
Council of Clermont
PS: 3, 9, 70–71
Courtly love
A: 174–75
Crusade of the Shepherds
PS: 110
Crusader castles, remains of
A: 187 (ill.)
Crusader states
A: 69–89
"The Crusaders in Mainz"
PS: 115, **117–19**

D

Damascus, siege of
A: 92, 93 (ill.)
Damietta, siege of
A: 108, 110 (ill.)
Dandolo, Enrico (doge of Venice)
A: 102–05
B: 14, 14 (ill.), 15
PS: 25–27
Danishmends
A: 71
Death of Arthur, The
A: 179
See also Morte d'Arthur
"Decline of Christian Power in the Holy Land, 1164: Letter from Aymeric, Patriarch of Antioch to Louis VII of France"
***PS:* 72–75**
Divine Comedy
A: 175
Dome of the Rock
A: 23 (ill.)
Ducas, Constantine
B: 68
Ducas, Irene
B: 67
Duqaq
A: 71

E

Eastern Orthodox (Greek Orthodox) Church,
A: 2, 12
B: 126
Eighty-Six Sermons on the Song of Songs
B: 59

Eleanor of Aquitaine
A: 36, 175 (ill.)
B: 63, **75–82,** 75 (ill.), 140, 172, 194
Elizabeth II
A: 134–35
Emico
PS: 115, 116, 117
Ephraim ben Jacob
B: 62
Epic of Kings, The
A: 169 (ill.)
Erec
A: 178
Etheria of Aquitaine
A: 36
Eugenius III, Pope
B: 61, 77
Eustace II
A: 84
B: 104, 105

F

"The Fall of Acre, 1291"
PS: **54–58**
Fatimids
A: 30, 49, 76, 87, 116
B: 25, 26, 110, 186
Ferdinand
A: 193
Feudalism
A: 137–38
Fifth Crusade
A: 107–10
B: 87–88, 96, 131–33
PS: 4–5, 33–34
First Crusade
A: 28–30, 52, 55, 60–61, 82–90
B: 6–8, 67, 70–72, 76, 77, 103, 105–10, 113, 165
PS: 3–4, 10–19, 70, 165
Fitzgerald, Edward
PS: 162
Foundation Stone
A: 5, 14
Fourth Crusade
A: 66–67, 101–07
B: 11, 14–18, 124–25, 130–31
PS: 4, 22–31, 75, 77, 167
Fourth Lateran Council
B: 127
Francis of Assisi
B: **83–91,** 83 (ill.), 89 (ill.), 133
PS: 34
Franciscans
B: 83, 87, 88–90
Franks
A: 8–10, 17, 28–32
Frederick I (Frederick Barbarossa)
A: 10, 96
Frederick II
A: 10, 28, 111–13, 194–95
B: 34, **93–101,** 93 (ill.), 123, 134–35
PS: 34–45, 34 (ill.), **36–39,** 37 (ill.)
Fulk V of Anjou
B: 118, 158, 159 (ill.)

G

Gate of David
A: 42
Geoffrey de Saint Omer
B: 116
Geoffrey de Villehardouin
PS: **24–28,** 25 (ill.)
Gerard de Martigues
B: 114
Gerold of Valence
PS: 35, **39–43**
"Gerold to All the Faithful"
PS: **39–43**
Godfrey of Bouillon
A: 84, 88
B: 6–7, 71, 98, **103–111,** 103 (ill.), 107 (ill.), 115
Goksu River
A: 97 (ill.)
Great Mosque
A: 17 (ill.)
Great Schism
A: 12–13
Gregory VII, Pope
A: 50, 59, 194–95
B: 122, 212–13
Gregory IX, Pope
B: 98–99
Guy of Lusignan
A: 66, 98
B: 162

H

Hakim
A: 26, 30, 35, 128
Hasan al-Sabah
A: 78
Hasan II
B: 205, 206
Helena
A: 26–27, 42
Henry I, of England
A: 9
Henry II, of England
A: 9
B: 79–80, 172
PS: **168–69** 166 (ill.)
Henry III
B: 80
Henry IV
B: 104, 213, 214
Henry VI
B: 13, 178
Heroic literature
A: 169–71
Historia rerum in partibus transmarinis gestarum (History of Deeds Done beyond the Sea)
A: 131 (ill.)
B: 72
Holy Lance
A: 86
Holy Land
A: 33–46
"The Holy Light: How it Descends Upon the Holy Sepulchre"
PS: 147–148, **151–54**
Holy Roman Empire
A: 10–11
B: 95
Hospital of Saint John
A: 42, 147 (ill.)
Hugh de Payens
B: 59, **113–20,** 113 (ill.)
Hugh of Vermandois
A: 84

Hulagu
A: 185
B: 41
Hussain ibn Ali
A: 73

I

Ibn al-Athir
B: 220
PS: 133–39, **136–39**
Ibn al-Baitar
B: 136
Ibn Said
PS: 98, **101–03**
Ibn Tufayl
B: 31
Ilghazi
A: 122
In Praise of the New Knighthood
B: 118
Indulgences
A: 54
PS: 76
Innocent II, Pope
B: 59–61
Innocent III, Pope
A: 63–64, 102, 107–08
B: 83, 86, 87, 94, **121–28,** 121 (ill.), 123 (ill.)
PS: 22, 29–30, 31, 75, 116, 167
Isaac II, Emperor
B: 12, 13, 16
PS: 25, 27–28
Isabella
A: 193
Isabella Yolanda
A: 111
Islam
A: 1–4, 13–18, 24
PS: 143–44, 145
Five Pillars of
B: 84
Israel
A: 200–01
Itinerary of Benjamin of Tudela: Travels in the Middle Ages
PS: **124–30**
Itzchaki, Shlomo (Rashi)
B: 149

J

Jaffe, count of
B: 158
Jaggar, Mick
A: 134-35
Jerome, Saint
A: 46
Jerusalem
A: 20–32, 34 (ill.)
battle for (1099)
A: 117 (ill.)
fall of
A: 95–99
PS: 48, 51–54
Jewish quarter of
A: 34 (ill.)
Kingdom of
A: 89–90
B: 156
medieval map of
A: 3 (ill.)
siege of
A: 87–89
B: 108–09
Jesus Christ (Jesus of Nazareth)
A: 6, 26, 33, 43
entry into Jerusalem
A: 21 (ill.)
Jews, persecution of
A: 125–33, 129 (ill.), 132 (ill.)
B: 176
PS: 115–32
Jihad
A: 79–80
B: 61
PS: 98, 104, 105
John, King of France
B: 178–79
John, King of Jerusalem
A: 108–11
PS: 33, 39
Joseph of Arimathea
A: 28, 43
Jousting
A: 142 (ill.)
Judaism
A: 4

K

Kalavun
P: 49
Kamil, al-Malik al-
B: 83, 88, 97, **129–36,** 195
PS: 33–34, 35, 37, 39, 41, 42, 43–45
Kerbogha
A: 71
Khalil, al-Ashraf
A: 190
B: 40
PS: 49
Kitab al-kulliyat ("Generalities")
B: 31
Kitab fasl al-maqal ("On the Harmony of Religion and Philosophy")
B: 32, 33
Kitbogha
B: 41, 43
Khwarismians
A: 28, 181
Knighthood
A: 134–38, 140–44
Knights
in battle
A: 161 (ill.)
traveling to the Holy Land
A: 61 (ill.), 143 (ill.)
Knights Hospitallers
A: 31, 42, 146–51, 185
B: 40, 43, 114
PS: 40, 48, 53, 54, 58, 59–60, 74, 167, 172
Knights of Malta
A: 150–51
Knights Templars
A: 31, 145 (ill.), 150 (ill.), 151–55, 185, 190
B: 40, 43, 59, 113, 116–19, 208
PS: 40, 41, 53, 54, 57, 58, 59, 74, 167, 170–71, 172
Koran
A: 13, 25, 198 (ill.)
PS: 147, **149–51** 151 (ill.)
Krak des Chevaliers
A: 149 (ill.), 162 (ill.)

L

Lancelot
A: 178
"*Las Siete Partidas:* Laws of the Jews"
PS: **119–24**
Lateran Councils
PS: 131
Lateran Palace
A: 107
Le Puy, Bishop of
A: 85
Leo III, Pope
A: 10
Leopold, Duke of Austria
A: 98–101
Lothair II
B: 60
Louis VI
A: 132 (ill.)
B: 76
Louis VII
A: 91, 92 (ill.), 93 (ill.), 123
B: 61, 76–79
Louis IX
A: 82 (ill.) 113, 181–85, 184 (ill.)
B: 39, **139–46**, 139 (ill.)
Ludolph of Suchem
PS: **54–58**

M

Magna Carta
A: 195
Maimonides
B: 48, **147–54**, 147 (ill.)
Malik al-Kamil
A: 28
See also Al-Kamil, al-Malik; Kamil, al-Malik al-
Malik-Shah
B: 23, 24, 27
Mamluks
A: 185–88
PS: 48, 141
Manuel Comnenus
B: 51, 52 (ill.)
Map of Christian Holy Lands
A: 37 (ill.)
Maracius
A: 26
Mary Magdalene
A: 43
Massoath Schel Rabbi Benjamin (The Itinerary of Benjamin of Tudela)
B: 47, 49, 54, 55
See Also **Itinerary of Benjamin of Tudela: Travels in the Middle Ages**
McCartney Paul,
A: 134–35
Mecca
A: 4, 13
Medina
A: 13–14, 15 (ill.)
Melisende
B: **155–62,** 159 (ill.)
Melot Spaheraph
PS: 54–55
Minnesängers
A: 174
Mishneh Torah ("Second Torah")
B: 147, 148, 150–152, 151 (ill.)
Mongols
A: 183
PS: 134–39, 135 (ill.), 138 (ill.), 141
Moors
A: 18
Moreh Nevuchim ("The Guide of the Perplexed")
B: 147, 152–53
Morte d'Arthur
A: 179
See also Death of Arthur, The
Mount Calvary
A: 43
Mount of Olives
A: 45
Muhammad
A: 13–14, 13 (ill.), 22, 24
Muhammad Shah
PS: 140
Muslim warriors
A: 70 (ill.)

N

Najm al-Din Ayyub, al- (also al-Salih Najm al-Din Ayyub)
B: 39, 41, 142, 184, 195
Nasir al-Din
B: 144
Nero
A: 107
Nicephorus III
B: 4
Nicodemus
A: 43
Niebelungenlied
A: 170
Nizam al-Mulk
B: 23
Nur al-Din
B: 160, 184–85, 186, 223
PS: 22, 104
See also Al-Din, Nur
Nureddin
PS: 73, 74

O

Odovacar
A: 7
Omar Khayyam
PS: 148–149, **160–161**
"On the Tatars"
PS: 134–39, **136–39**
Otto I
A: 10
Otto IV
B: 94–95

P

Palestinian children
A: 200 (ill.)
Paper
B: 34
Parzival
A: 179
Paula of Bethlehem, Saint
A: 46
Pelagius, Cardinal
A: 108–09
B: 131–32, 133
Penance
A: 36–37
People's Crusade
A: 54–56
B: 166–69

PS: 9–10, 69, 110
Pepin the Short
A: 8
Percival; or, The Story of the Grail
A: 178 (ill.)
Peter the Hermit
A: 54–55, 132 (ill.)
B: 6, 71, **163–70**
PS: 9–10, 69, 165
Philip II
A: 96–99, 158 (ill.)
B: 172–73, 174, 178–79, 190
Philip IV
A: 154
Philip of Swabia
B: 13
Pilgrimages
A: 33–46
"Poem on the Crusades"
PS: **100–01**
Prester John
B: 78–79
Primogeniture
A: 60
"The Prior Who Became a Moslem"
PS: 148, **154–60**
"Profession of Faith"
PS: 148, **160–61**

Q

Qalawun, al-Mansur
A: 189–90
Qutuz, Saif al-Din
A: 186–87
B: 42–43

R

Ramleh
A: 41–42
Raymond, count of St. Gilles
B: 78–79
PS: 14, 74
Raymond of Toulouse
A: 76, 85–86
B: 105, 110
Reynald de Châtillon
A: 95
B: 188
Richard I (Lionheart)
A: 59, 60 (ill.), 66, 96–101, 123 (ill.), 124
B: 80–81, **171–81,** 171 (ill.), 190–91, 209
PS: 22
Richard II, Duke of Normandy
A: 35
Ridwan
A: 79
Robert Guiscard
B: 3, 4
Robert of Artois
B: 143
Robert of Flanders
B: 5, 105
Roger de Flor
B: 40
Roman Catholic Church
B: 126
Roman Empire
A: 2, 5–7, 10
Romance
A: 175–80
Romanus IV Diogenes
A: 49
B: 3, 25, 26
The Rubaiyat of Omar Khayyam
PS: 162

S

Saladin
A: 28, 66, 94, 96–101, 123 (ill.), 124
B: 39, 53, 54, 55, 98, 129, 150, 174, **183–92,** 183 (ill.), 207, 224
PS: 22, 104
"The Saladin Tithe"
A: 98
PS: 166, **168–69**
Schirkuh
PS: 73
Second Crusade
A: 90–94
B: 50, 57, 58, 61–63, 75, 77–79, 81, 155, 160
PS: 22, 70, 77, 107–10
Second Temple
A: 5–6
Sefer Zechirah ("Book of Memoirs")
B: 62
Seljuks
A: 48–52, 71, 75, 116, 119–21, 120 (ill.)
B: 106–07
PS: 1–2
Sephardim
B: 48
Seventh Crusade
A: 113–14, 183–84
B: 30, 197–98
PS: 5, 49–59
Shahnameh
A: 169 (ill.)
Shajarat al-Durr
B: 39, 41, 143, **193–201**
Shiites
A: 72, 116, 119–20
B: 55, 204–05
PS: 98
Shirkuh,
B: 186
Shroud of Turin
B: 17
Sinan, Rashid al-Din
B: **203–10**
Sir Gawain and the Green Knight
A: 178
Sirat Baybars
B: 44
Sixth Crusade
A: 10, 110–13, 194–95
B: 93–94, 97–98, 129, 134–35
PS: 34–45, 76, 77
Solomon bar Samson
PS: 115, **117–19**
Song of Roland
A: 172 (ill.)
PS: 80–91, **82–91**
See also Chanson de Roland
Stephen of Blois
PS: **10–15,** 18

"Stephen, Count of Blois and Chartres, to His Wife Adele"
PS: 12–15
Stephen of Cloyes
PS: 30–31
Sunnis
A: 72, 75, 77, 116, 119
B: 22, 204–05
PS: 97
Sybille
B: 162

T

Tahafut al-falasifa ("The Incoherence of Philosophers)
B: 32
Tahafut al-tahafut ("The Incoherence of Incoherence")
B: 29, 32
Tancred
A: 61
B: 177
Taticius
PS: 16
Temple of Solomon
A: 5, 14
Teutonic Knights
A: 155
PS: 56, 58, 167, 170–71
Theodosius I
A: 6–7
Third Crusade
A: 10, 96–101
B: 12–18, 62, 130, 174–78, 183, 190–91
Tolord de Melaye
PS: 51–54
Tomb of the Mamluks
A: 186 (ill.)
Tomb of the Virgin
A: 45
Treaty of Jaffa
A: 28, 112–13
Treaty of Ramlah,
B: 191
Tripoli, taking of
A: 77 (ill.)
Troubadours
A: 174
PS: 81, 93 (ill.), 94
Trouvères
A: 174
True Cross 27 (ill.),
A: 28, 42, 44 (ill.), 108, 127 (ill.)
Tughril Beg
B: 22
Tunisia
A: 75 (ill.)
Turan Shah
B: 39, 41, 197–98

U

Umar
A: 16, 23
Umayyads
A: 72
Urban II, Pope
A: 1, 52, 53 (ill.), 59, 83–84, 142
B: 1, 6, 27, 104, 115, 163, 165, 167, **211–18**, 211 (ill.)
PS: 2–3, 9, 67, **70–71**
"Speech at the Council of Clermont, 1095"
PS: 70–71
Urban VI, Pope
PS: 60
Urfa
A: 62 (ill.)
Usamah ibn Munqidh
B: 219–25
Uthman
A: 72

V

Via Dolorosa
A: 42
Victor III, Pope
B: 213
Violence
A: 139–40

W

Walter the Penniless
PS: 10
Warfare
A: 157–67
weapons used during
A: 159 (ill.), 163 (ill.), 165 (ill.)
William, Duke of Normandy
A: 9
William IX
B: 76
PS: 95
William of Beaujeau
PS: 55
William of Rubruck
A: 183
William X
B: 76
Women Crusaders
A: 36

Y

Yolande
B: 96–97
Yussuf Kothual
B: 26
Yvain
A: 178

Z

Zealots
A: 5
Zengi, Imad al-Din
A: 90–91, 122
B: 61, 77, 155, 160, 184–85, 186
PS: 21–22, 104, 107